MYSTERY IN LONDON

It is the year 1898 in London. You are Mycroft Pound, the famous detective and you must find the Whitechapel Killer. He attacks people with a long knife and six women are dead because of him.

Now another woman is lying in the street, outside the Rose and Crown. There is blood everywhere and she is very ill. You see bicycle tracks on the road. What do you do? Do you follow the bicycle tracks, or do you talk to the people in the Rose and Crown? Be careful – there is only one way to catch the Whitechapel Killer. But you must move quickly – before the killer escapes and kills again.

This is an interactive story. You can choose what part of the story to read next. Follow the numbers at the end of each section.

OXFORD BOOKWORMS LIBRARY

Crime & Mystery

Mystery in London

Starter (250 headwords)

HELEN BROOKE

Mystery in London

Illustrated by
Ron Tiner

OXFORD UNIVERSITY PRESS

OXFORD
UNIVERSITY PRESS

Great Clarendon Street, Oxford OX2 6DP

Oxford University Press is a department of the University of Oxford.
It furthers the University's objective of excellence in research, scholarship,
and education by publishing worldwide in

Oxford New York

Auckland Cape Town Dar es Salaam Hong Kong Karachi
Kuala Lumpur Madrid Melbourne Mexico City Nairobi
New Delhi Shanghai Taipei Toronto

With offices in

Argentina Austria Brazil Chile Czech Republic France Greece
Guatemala Hungary Italy Japan Poland Portugal Singapore
South Korea Switzerland Thailand Turkey Ukraine Vietnam

OXFORD and OXFORD ENGLISH are registered trade marks of
Oxford University Press in the UK and in certain other countries

ISBN: 978 0 19 423428 3

Printed in China

Word count (main text): 1450

For more information on the Oxford Bookworms Library, visit
www.oup.com/bookworms

This book is printed on paper from certified and well-managed sources.

CONTENTS

Mystery in London

1 It is the year 1898, and you are Mycroft Pound, the famous detective. You are sitting in your house in London, one cold November evening. There is a knock at the door. It is Inspector Freewell of the London police.

'Can you come to Whitechapel, Mr Pound? We need your help. There's a woman in the street. She isn't dead, but there's blood everywhere. We think it's the Whitechapel Killer again.'

■ *You put on your coat. Go to* **18.**

2 You are in Annie's house. A woman comes in.

'Who are you? What are you doing here?' she asks.

You tell her about Annie.

'That's terrible,' she says.

'Do you know any of her friends?' you ask.

The woman thinks. 'Her best friend is a woman called Rosy. She lives in Limehouse Street. But she has a boyfriend. That's him, there, in that picture. I don't like him.'

■ *You go back to the Rose and Crown to talk to the other people. Go to* **10**.

■ *You go to Limehouse Street to look for Rosy. Go to* **35**.

3 You want to get on to the *Californian* and talk to Jack.

■ *You jump in the water and swim after the ship. Go to* **8**.

■ *You cannot swim. You think about how you can get on to the ship. Go to* **13**.

4 'Do you know the name of the woman in the street?' you ask the old man.

He cannot hear you and he does not answer.

■ *Go to* **10**.

5 You go across the bridge, but you cannot see the *Californian*. There is a sailor in one of the small boats, and there is an old man fishing.

■ *You ask the sailor for help. Go to* **24.**
■ *You ask the old man for help. Go to* **34.**

6 You talk to the young man. He comes into the street and looks at the woman.

'Her name's Annie, I think,' he says.

'Do you know where she lives?'

'Yes. She lives in Cable Street, I think.'

■ You go *back into the Rose and Crown and talk to the other people. Go to* **10.**

■ You go to *Cable Street. Go to* **30.**

7 The captain of the *Californian* calls the three Jacks. Which Jack do you want to speak to?

■ *The Jack on the left. Go to* **17.**
■ *The Jack in the middle. Go to* **23.**
■ *The Jack on the right. Go to* **31.**

8 You jump into the water and swim after the ship. But the ship is going very fast. After five minutes, the *Californian* is out of the London docks and going to India. And you are now very cold.

■ *Go to* **22.**

9 You tell Rosy about Annie.

'I'm Annie's best friend,' she says. She is crying. 'But she has a boyfriend.'

'Who's he?' you ask.

'A sailor. His name's Jack. He's often at her house in Cable Street. His ship's in the London docks now, I think.'

■ *You want to find Jack, so you go to the docks. Go to* **14.**

■ *You want to find out more about Annie so you go to her house in Cable Street. Go to* **19.**

10 There are four people in the Rose and Crown. You want to ask some questions about the woman in the street. Who do you talk to first?

■ *You talk to the old man. Go to* **4.**
■ *You talk to the young man. Go to* **6.**
■ *You talk to the old woman. Go to* **15.**
■ *You talk to the young woman. Go to* **28.**

11 The sailor looks at you.

'Jack?' he says. 'There are hundreds of sailors called Jack. There's a Jack on every ship.'

You must find the name of Jack's ship. You go to Annie's room to look for more information.

■ *Go to* **19**.

12 You are in the London docks. There are hundreds of ships. You want to find the *Californian* and you want to catch Jack.

■ *You go across the bridge.* Go to **5**.

■ *You go to the right.* Go to **20**.

■ *You go to the left.* Go to **29**.

13 There is a bridge across the water. You go on the bridge and jump onto the *Californian*. You go to the captain.

'There's a man on your ship I must talk to,' you say. 'His name is Jack.'

'Why do you want to talk to him?' he asks.

'He's the Whitechapel Killer, I think.'

'There are three Jacks on my ship,' says the captain.

'Can I see them all?' you ask.

■ *Go to 7.*

14 You go to the London docks to look for Jack, Annie's friend. There are hundreds of ships, and thousands of sailors. You talk to a sailor.

'Do you know a sailor called Jack?' you ask.

■ *Go to* **11.**

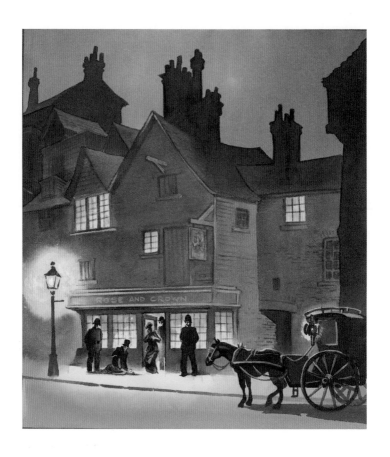

15 You talk to the old woman. She comes into the street and looks at the woman.

'Her name's Annie,' she says.

'Do you know where she lives?' you ask.

'Yes. She lives in Cable Street. I don't know what number,' she answers.

■ *You go back to the Rose and Crown and talk to the other people. Go to* **10**.

■ *You go to Cable Street. Go to* **30**.

16 You knock at the white door. A young woman opens the door.

'Are you Rosy?' you ask.

'Yes.'

'Are you a friend of Annie?'

'Yes,' she says.

'I've got bad news for you,' you say. 'I'm afraid she's very ill.'

'No.' Rosy starts to cry.

■ *Go to* **9.**

17 You talk to the Jack on the left. He is not the Whitechapel Killer.

■ *Go to 7.*

18 The Whitechapel Killer attacks people with a long knife. Six women are dead because of him.

You arrive in Whitechapel and the police are waiting for you there. The woman is lying in the street, near the Rose and Crown. She is very ill, so she cannot talk to you. You see some bicycle tracks on the road.

■ *You follow the bicycle tracks. Go to* **25.**

■ *You go into the Rose and Crown. You want to talk to the people there. Go to* **10.**

19 You look in Annie's house and find a letter.

The Californian, Saturday

Annie,

Tomorrow my ship is going to India. Please meet me at the Rose and Crown tonight. I have something very important for you.

Jack

So the name of Jack's ship is the *Californian*. Is Jack the man you want? Is Jack the Whitechapel Killer? You go to the London docks to look for Jack on the *Californian*.

■ *Go to* **12.**

20 There are a lot of ships, but you cannot see the *Californian* here.

■ *Go back to 12.*

21 You knock on the blue door. An old man opens it. 'I'm looking for Rosy,' you say.

'She doesn't live here,' he says. 'She lives in the white house, I think.'

■ *Go to 16.*

22 The Whitechapel Killer is free. Can you be a better detective next time? Try again.

■ *Go back to* **1**.

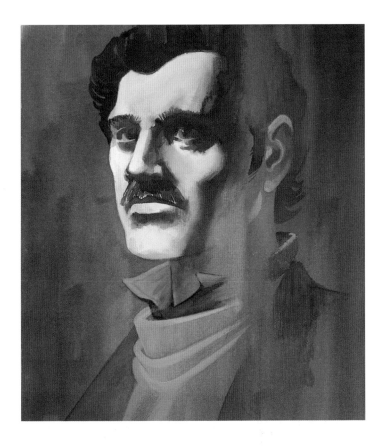

23 You talk to the Jack in the middle. He is not the Whitechapel Killer.

■ *Go to* **7**.

24 You talk to the sailor.

'Do you know a ship called the *Californian*?' you ask him.

The sailor looks at you. 'I am from Russia,' he says. 'I do not speak English.'

■ *Go to 5.*

25 You follow the bicycle tracks to a bigger road, so you cannot see the tracks any more.

■ *Go to 18.*

26 You knock on the red door. There is no-one at home.

■ *Go to 35.*

27 There is a knife in his pocket. And there is blood on it. This Jack is the Whitechapel Killer.

■ *Go to 33.*

28 'Do you know the name of the woman in the street?' you ask the young woman in the Rose and Crown. She comes out into the street and looks at her. 'I don't know her name but she has a friend called Rosy. Ask her!'

'Where does Rosy live?' you ask.

'She lives in Limehouse Street.'

■ *You go back to the Rose and Crown and talk to the other people. Go to* **10.**

■ *You go to Limehouse Street to find Rosy. Go to* **35.**

29 You go to the East India Dock. You can see the *Californian*, but it is sailing out of the dock.

■ *You can see Jack so you try to get on the ship. Go to* **3.**

■ *You cannot see Jack on the ship. You can go to the hospital and talk to Annie, and you can write to the Indian police about Jack. Go to* **22.**

30 You go to Cable Street, and talk to the people there. After a few minutes you find Annie's house. You look at everything very carefully.

■ *Go to 2.*

31 You talk to the Jack on the right.

'Do you know a woman called Annie?' you ask.

'No,' he says.

But this Jack has an ear-ring. And there is something in his pocket. Is it a knife? Perhaps this Jack is the Whitechapel Killer.

■ *Go to 27.*

32 Another good day's work for Mycroft Pound, the great detective, finishes. You go back to your house. No criminal is safe in London when Mycroft, the great detective, is at work.

33 The captain helps you, and you arrest the Whitechapel Killer. You take him off the ship and give him to the police.

■ *Go to 32.*

34 You talk to the old man.

'Do you know a ship called the *Californian*?' you ask him.

'Yes,' he says. 'It's going to India today, so it's in the East India Dock.'

You must find the East India Dock.

■ *Go to 12.*

35 You go to Limehouse Street. You are looking for Rosy, Annie's friend. Which house do you want to try first?

■ *The house with the white door. Go to* **16.**
■ *The house with the blue door. Go to* **21.**
■ *The house with the red door. Go to* **26.**

GLOSSARY

attack try to hurt someone

blood red liquid inside the body

criminal a person who breaks the law

detective a person who tries to find criminals

ear-ring a metal circle people wear in their ears

famous a famous person is someone who many people know

free not in prison

great very clever or important

jump move quickly into or onto something

killer a person who kills other people

knife something you use to cut things

knock hit a door to tell people that you are outside

letter you send a letter to someone by post

news information in a newspaper, on the radio or television

safe not in danger

sailor a person who works on ships

ship something people use to travel across the sea

swim move your body through water using your arms and legs

terrible very bad

track the mark something leaves on the road

Mystery in London

ACTIVITIES

Before Reading

1 **Look at the front and back cover of the book and choose the correct ending for these sentences.**

  1 The story happens . . .
    a ☐ about twenty years ago.
    b ☐ about fifty years ago.
    c ☐ about a hundred years ago.

  2 Mycroft Pound is . . .
    a ☐ a doctor.
    b ☐ a teacher.
    c ☐ a detective.

2 **Guess what happens. For each sentence choose one answer.**

	YES	NO
1 Somebody kills a rich man.	☐	☐
2 The police put Mycroft Pound in prison.	☐	☐
3 The police put the Whitechapel Killer in prison.	☐	☐
4 Mycroft Pound catches the Whitechapel Killer.	☐	☐

ACTIVITIES

While Reading

1 **Read the first two parts of the story (1 and 18).**
Are these sentences true (T) or false (F)?

	T	F
1 The story is in the summer.	☐	☐
2 At the beginning of the story, Mycroft Pound is at home.	☐	☐
3 The police come to Mycroft Pound's home.	☐	☐
4 A woman is dead in the street.	☐	☐
5 The woman is in the Rose and Crown.	☐	☐
6 The Whitechapel Killer uses a knife.	☐	☐
7 There is a bicycle near the woman.	☐	☐
8 There are bicycle tracks near the woman.	☐	☐

2 **What next? Where next?**
Complete the following sentences.

1 The bicycle tracks go . . .
  a ☐ nowhere.
  b ☐ to the killer's house.
  c ☐ to the woman's house.

2 In the Rose and Crown Mycroft finds . . .
  a ☐ nobody.
  b ☐ a lot of people.
  c ☐ a few people.

3 In the Rose and Crown people are . . .
   a ☐ singing.
   b ☐ drinking beer.
   c ☐ reading.

4 The woman . . .
   a ☐ dies.
   b ☐ does not die.

5 The Whitechapel Killer is . . .
   a ☐ a dog.
   b ☐ a woman.
   c ☐ a man.

6 The woman cannot talk . . .
   a ☐ because she is dying.
   b ☐ because she is ill.
   c ☐ because she is afraid.

After Reading

1 Answer these questions.

Who

1 . . . asks Mycroft for help at the beginning of the story?
2 . . . talks to the people in the Rose and Crown?
3 . . . lives in Cable Street?
4 . . . lives in a house with a white door?
5 . . . is going to India on a ship?
6 . . . jumps onto the *Californian*?

2 Who says this? Who do they say it to?

1 'I'm Annie's best friend.' .... says this to ....
2 'There's a man on your ship I must talk to.' .... says this to ....
3 'Can you come to Whitechapel?' .... says this to ....

3 Complete this summary of the story. Use these words:

boyfriend detective jumps London name police
sailor ship street talks tell woman

Mycroft Pound is a famous .... , who lives in ....
One day the .... ask him to help them; a .... is lying

in the .... in Whitechapel in front of the Rose and
Crown. Mycroft goes to Whitechapel and .... to the
people in the Rose and Crown. They .... Mycroft that
the woman's .... is Annie. Annie lives in Cable Street,
so Mycroft goes to her house. A woman tells him that Annie
has a ....; his name is Jack and he is a .... Mycroft
goes to the London Docks to find Jack. Jack's .... , the
Californian, is leaving, but Mycroft .... on to the ship.
He finds Jack, and gives him to the police.

4 There are three Jacks on the *Californian*. Write a description
of Jack, the Whitechapel Killer.

....
....
....
....
....

ABOUT THE AUTHOR

Helen Brooke was born in the north of England. She has worked in many different jobs, in many different countries, all around the world. She now lives near Oxford in England. She is very interested in interactive reading. She has also written *Survive!* (Starter) for the Oxford Bookworms Library.

OXFORD BOOKWORMS LIBRARY

Classics • Crime & Mystery • Factfiles • Fantasy & Horror
Human Interest • Playscripts • Thriller & Adventure
True Stories • World Stories

The OXFORD BOOKWORMS LIBRARY provides enjoyable reading in English, with a wide range of classic and modern fiction, non-fiction, and plays. It includes original and adapted texts in seven carefully graded language stages, which take learners from beginner to advanced level. An overview is given on the next pages.

All Stage 1 titles are available as audio recordings, as well as over eighty other titles from Starter to Stage 6. All Starters and many titles at Stages 1 to 4 are specially recommended for younger learners. Every Bookworm is illustrated, and Starters and Factfiles have full-colour illustrations.

The OXFORD BOOKWORMS LIBRARY also offers extensive support. Each book contains an introduction to the story, notes about the author, a glossary, and activities. Additional resources include tests and worksheets, and answers for these and for the activities in the books. There is advice on running a class library, using audio recordings, and the many ways of using Oxford Bookworms in reading programmes. Resource materials are available on the website <www.oup.com/bookworms>.

The *Oxford Bookworms Collection* is a series for advanced learners. It consists of volumes of short stories by well-known authors, both classic and modern. Texts are not abridged or adapted in any way, but carefully selected to be accessible to the advanced student.

You can find details and a full list of titles in the *Oxford Bookworms Library Catalogue* and *Oxford English Language Teaching Catalogues*, and on the website <www.oup.com/bookworms>.

THE OXFORD BOOKWORMS LIBRARY
GRADING AND SAMPLE EXTRACTS

STARTER • 250 HEADWORDS

present simple – present continuous – imperative –
can/cannot, must – *going to* (future) – simple gerunds …

Her phone is ringing – but where is it?

Sally gets out of bed and looks in her bag. No phone. She looks under the bed. No phone. Then she looks behind the door. There is her phone. Sally picks up her phone and answers it. *Sally's Phone*

STAGE 1 • 400 HEADWORDS

… past simple – coordination with *and*, *but*, *or* –
subordination with *before*, *after*, *when*, *because*, *so* …

I knew him in Persia. He was a famous builder and I worked with him there. For a time I was his friend, but not for long. When he came to Paris, I came after him – I wanted to watch him. He was a very clever, very dangerous man. *The Phantom of the Opera*

STAGE 2 • 700 HEADWORDS

… present perfect – *will* (future) – *(don't) have to, must not, could* –
comparison of adjectives – simple *if* clauses – past continuous –
tag questions – *ask/tell* + infinitive …

While I was writing these words in my diary, I decided what to do. I must try to escape. I shall try to get down the wall outside. The window is high above the ground, but I have to try. I shall take some of the gold with me – if I escape, perhaps it will be helpful later. *Dracula*

… should, may – present perfect continuous – *used to* – past perfect –
causative – relative clauses – indirect statements …

Of course, it was most important that no one should see Colin, Mary, or Dickon entering the secret garden. So Colin gave orders to the gardeners that they must all keep away from that part of the garden in future. ***The Secret Garden***

STAGE 4 • 1400 HEADWORDS
… past perfect continuous – passive (simple forms) –
would conditional clauses – indirect questions –
relatives with *where/when* – gerunds after prepositions/phrases …

I was glad. Now Hyde could not show his face to the world again. If he did, every honest man in London would be proud to report him to the police. ***Dr Jekyll and Mr Hyde***

STAGE 5 • 1800 HEADWORDS
… future continuous – future perfect –
passive (modals, continuous forms) –
would have conditional clauses – modals + perfect infinitive …

If he had spoken Estella's name, I would have hit him. I was so angry with him, and so depressed about my future, that I could not eat the breakfast. Instead I went straight to the old house. ***Great Expectations***

STAGE 6 • 2500 HEADWORDS
… passive (infinitives, gerunds) – advanced modal meanings –
clauses of concession, condition

When I stepped up to the piano, I was confident. It was as if I knew that the prodigy side of me really did exist. And when I started to play, I was so caught up in how lovely I looked that I didn't worry how I would sound. ***The Joy Luck Club***

Oranges in the Snow

PHILLIP BURROWS AND MARK FOSTER

'Everything's ready now. We can do the experiment,' says your assistant Joe.

You are the famous scientist Mary Durie working in a laboratory in Alaska. When you discover something very new and valuable, other people want to try to steal your idea – can you stop them before they escape?

Survive!

HELEN BROOKE

You are in a small plane, going across the Rocky Mountains. Suddenly, the engine starts to make strange noises . . .

Soon you are alone, in the snow, at the top of a mountain, and it is very, very cold. Can you find your way out of the mountain?

BOOKWORMS · THRILLER & ADVENTURE · STARTER

Drive into Danger

ROSEMARY BORDER

'I can drive a truck,' says Kim on her first day at work in the office. When Kim's passenger Andy finds something strange under the truck things get dangerous – very dangerous.

BOOKWORMS · CRIME & MYSTERY · STARTER

Give us the Money

MAEVE CLARKE

'Every day is the same. Nothing exciting ever happens to me,' thinks Adam one boring Monday morning. But today is not the same. When he helps a beautiful young woman because some men want to take her bag, life gets exciting and very, very dangerous.

Sherlock Holmes and the Duke's Son

SIR ARTHUR CONAN DOYLE

Retold by Jennifer Bassett

Dr Huxtable has a school for boys in the north of England. When the Duke of Holdernesse decides to send his young son there, that is good news for the school. The Duke is a very important person, and Dr Huxtable is happy to have his son in the school.

But two weeks later Dr Huxtable is the unhappiest man in England. Why? And why does he take the train down to London and go to Baker Street? Why does he need the help of the famous detective Sherlock Holmes?

Because someone has kidnapped the Duke's son . . .

Sister Love and Other Crime Stories

JOHN ESCOTT

Some sisters are good friends, some are not. Sometimes there is more hate in a family than there is love. Karin is beautiful and has lots of men friends, but she can be very unkind to her sister Marcia. Perhaps when they were small, there was love between them, but that was a long time ago.

They say that everybody has one crime in them. Perhaps they only take an umbrella that does not belong to them. Perhaps they steal from a shop, perhaps they get angry and hit someone, perhaps they kill . . .